Secrets of Not Giving a Fuck

Berger McDonald

Secrets of Not Giving a Fuck

ISBN-13: 978-1979652520
ISBN-10: 197965252X

First Edition: November 2017
10 9 8 7 6 5 4 3 2 1

CONTENTS

What the fuck is this book about?

Life isn't always easy, unless of course you are an Instagram travel blogger who pretends it is.

We are living in a society now where literally our entire life is online; things such as your age, favorite color, the home-cooked meal nobody cares about, or who you hang out with last night, are all out there for the world to see. With a passive way of communicating, when we come across any criticism, it can ruin our day, make us paranoid or even cause us to delete our social media accounts completely.

Why do we give a fuck?

With more technological advancement comes less real

social interaction, and thus our abilities in dealing with real-life are becoming stunted.

More and more people are forgetting how to actually communicate in the real world and they turn into sensitive introverts, unable to get over small problems, let alone cope when serious shit hits the fan.

Turn on your TV or radio, watch a video on your phone or even read a newspaper and you will likely be met with unrealistic expectations that are commonplace now and they are the central contributor to the misery many people experience.

Once in a while, things happen, things you can't always control such as rain on your wedding day or needing to take a shit during a 2-hour job interview, but what if there was a way to train your mind to not give a fuck?

The over-stimulating appeal of how to better our lives only reminds us of what we think we are lacking. When was the last time you walked home from work, but stopped for a second to appreciate that it was a beautiful day?

This book is not just a self-help guide, it's a self-awareness strategy, to teach you that instead of spending hours, days, and weeks worrying about so many things, you can choose to simply not give a fuck.

What you can expect from this book

While there are numerous self-help books readily available, this book is written with the intent of empowering you so that you can start to take control of your life and stop worrying about so much shit.

Are you still feeling like, *"Well, I could certainly give less of a fuck, but I still don't know how."*

Do you wonder if this book is right for you?

You shouldn't read this book if:

- You are living a comfortable life with no challenges, and you have a "probably couldn't happen" mindset.

- You think it's normal to stare at your social media platforms for hours after a post, waiting for instant gratification.

- You are content in weekly debates with family about how to change your life.

- You always say yes at work when really you should say no.

- Your idea of dealing with problems involves drinking heavily, taking drugs or binging on Netflix.

- You are a big silly goose.

* * *

If you are thinking there is no way you are the type of person above, and:

- You are tired of stressing about attending social events because you don't feel good enough.

- You want to learn how to deal with criticism or negativity in a way that won't make you lose sleep.

- You have an idea, dream or goal but feel hesitant about pursuing it.

- You want to organize those things you give a fuck about and become better at managing them.

- You are ready to make changes but need the self-motivation to get there.

- You know somewhere within you lies a badass who won't take no for an answer.

Then this book is for you!

In this book, you will learn the best secrets of when to give a fuck, but most importantly, train yourself to know exactly when and how to NOT give a fuck so you can live a better life.

You will learn about:

- The top 10 things I personally don't give a fuck about and you shouldn't either

- The step by step method to categorize your fucks into the list so you know exactly when they happen to apply your "not giving a fuck" mentality

- How to face fear and accept your vulnerabilities so you don't have to give out so many unnecessary fucks

- All the pain in the ass at work such as how to not give a fuck at a meeting, the types of co-workers and how to not give a fuck about them, or how to handle your aggressive and bullying boss in a "not giving a fuck" way

- The joy of family and how to not give a fuck when needed

- and so much, much more...

Is anything above resonating with you?

If Yes, then congratulations!

Turn to the next page and let's start to not give a fuck and have a stress-free life!

Chapter 1: Cry at my Funeral

Most never think about their funeral, most can't even think about what to eat for lunch, but if you take a few steps back and consider the following, then your ability for giving a fuck should transition to inability to give a fuck.

On average, a research study shows that ten people will cry at your funeral. However, the biggest factor on whether someone will attend your burial is ultimately based on... the weather. If it rains, only a third of the people will show up.

Are you serious? After working so hard all your life, pleasing so many people, contributing so much to this world, giving a fuck so much, and in the end there are only ten people that will cry at your funeral, and even that number is seriously threatened by the weather?

It sounds shocking, especially when you think about

how every burial scene in Hollywood involves rain.

"You can have money piled to the ceiling but the size of your funeral is still going to depend on the weather." Chuck Tanner, American Baseball player and wise guy.

So, the moment you're thinking about giving a fuck about a person, stop for a second and ask yourself this question:

"Would this person cry at my funeral?"

If the answer is no, then you now know when to not give a fuck.

By the way, if the idea that nobody will cry frightens you, don't allow this to cause concern. Remember, this book is about not giving a fuck, if you really wanted you could just hire someone on fiverr.com to cry at your funeral.

For hundreds of years in Ireland, anytime somebody with a specific family name or someone of notoriety died, a group of women would sing at the funeral. You have probably heard of the term 'Banshee', in Irish folklore, it's believed that these women's spirits still accompany those families, screaming outside their homes to forewarn that someone is about to die.

Would you really want that at your funeral? I mean, a group of essentially strangers singing at your funeral because you were well known. If the hot Irish singers (who sound like Enya on helium) weren't there, would anyone actually still attend? Keep in mind, it rains pretty much every day in Ireland, so much that when the sun is out, it's becomes a national holiday.

So, if you think that a few of your friends wouldn't cry or even show up at your funeral, then why should you care. Now, apply this to every other aspect of your life.

- If I moved to a new city, what would my friends or family think?

- If I started a new job, what would my friends or family think?

- If I decided to get married to someone off of craigslist for visa purposes, would anyone raise an eyebrow or passively give a 'like' on social media?

If they don't care (especially if you got married) then

why should you care either?

The infamous Steve Jobs was noted for looking in the mirror every morning and asking himself, "What if I was to die today?" With confronting yourself about your own mortality, a few realizations may occur.

- You are reminded that you have nothing to lose since the worst case scenario is death

- You are reminded that the opinions of others are irrelevant when it comes to finding your own happiness

- You are reminded that you are alive now and thus can set the wheels in motion to achieve goals or make a dream become a reality.

What else should you not give a fuck about?

The list of things to NOT give a fuck about is endless, and initially we might not even acknowledge that something or someone is holding us back.

So how do I know what to not give a fuck about? Here's a list of ideas to get started.

- Your ex and who they are dating.

- When someone tells you to lose weight.

- Being friends with people you don't actually like on social media.

- Unable to buy the latest smartphone.

- Getting a tan.

- Comparing yourself to someone who makes more money.

- When someone you know gets married and you

didn't get an invite.

- Not being invited to any party organized by friends or acquaintances.

- Finding out how much someone makes.

- Negative film reviews of movies you loved.

- Whether your hobbies make you more masculine or feminine.

- Peer-pressured into starting some new digital fad.

- Peer-pressured into a diet.

- Married friends asking why are you still single.

- Eating pizza for breakfast.

- How many followers you have on twitter.

- Getting lost in IKEA and then having to ask for directions.

- Eating salads on the first date.

- Going on a date and they look nothing like their tinder profile so you proceed to go to the toilet and escape out the window, James Bond style.

- Internet trolls commenting on the way you look.

- Keeping up with the Joneses; creating a fake reality of your own life to appease others.

- Sticking to a diet.

- Chasing after people.

- Being considered cool or smart.

- Sticking to one job in fear of failure.

- Thinking yourself too old to learn a new skill such as breakdancing or twerking.

- Watching TV for three hours a day.

- Spending time somewhere you no longer enjoy.

- Spending time with people who don't mentally stimulate you.

- Family members who are desperate for you to get married or settle down.

- Sex tips.

- Who your partner is messaging.

- And so much more.

* * *

"Life is more fun when you stop caring what other people think." Blake Mycoskie, Businessman who clearly stopped giving a fuck.

* * *

Chapter 2: Your Fucking List

10 things that I personally don't give a fuck about and you shouldn't either

Deciding on the things you personally don't give a fuck about sounds as straight-forward as cleaning out a basement for a garage sale.

You look at things from your past and decide, "I don't need this in my life anymore," and throw them out.

Just by taking action, you are already well on your way to fixing your miserable life, but what are the main contenders that are causing problems?

Here are the ten things that used to cause so much stress in my life. The moment I decided to stop giving a fuck about them, everything changed.

1. The little nuisances that make a stressful job

It's rare in life to come across someone who loves their job, but you have to take into consideration how they possibly got to that point. Was it hard work, luck, sleeping with a manager or a combination of them all?

A waitress with a 'I don't give a fuck' mentality is more likely to be raking in a fortune in tips since she focuses on the positive aspects of her job; talking to customers, exercise from walking around all the time, flexible hours, etc. If she doesn't like the job, she knows there are plenty of other places she can work and enjoy her life.

A guy called Mark worked in customer service for a few years. His job was dealing with complaints and providing assistance. Sounds like a shit job, right? Well, Mark used to hate his job, up until he figured out that the customers weren't upset with him, and that often when he helped resolve the situations, they apologized profusely.

2. Scared of your boss

A difficult boss can cause us a great deal of stress and make you wonder if there is anything you can do to ease the suffering of being their modern-day slave. Why yes there is... don't give a fuck.

The moment your boss opts to delegate you yet another mediocre assignment, tell them no. Explain that you know what you are capable of and that you are sick of feeling undermined and underappreciated.

"But, what if he fires me?" Stop right there for starters. You're being scared right now. You're giving a fuck. The point of this book is stop that. Stop giving a fuck.

There is always the possibility that you are also stressing about your boss, but it's simply an over-exaggeration. Once and for all, man up and stop him from pushing you around, and you will be surprised how the situation will turn out to be much better for both of you.

3. Your gossiping co-workers

The biggest problem with co-workers usually involves gossip or being afraid that some of the skanks in admin are talking about you behind your back on their smoke break.

You could try and engage in conversation with their primitive low-level English, or simply just not give a fuck and feel content that you don't have time for them.

4. Your financial situation

If you stress about being unable to afford something, or you don't have enough money to go out and visit friends then stop right now. If you think you can find other sources of income then do it, and if not, then it's out of your control and as such there is no point in stressing.

A friend of mine who recently lost his job wasn't fazed by the fact that he had to budget, in fact he used to joke about inviting his friends over for some hot water and stale bread. In the time he waited for an interview, he spent time reading and seeing old friends, utilizing time he hadn't had before to better himself. The situation wasn't great but his attitude and the way he reacted was. You see, he knew there was no point of giving a fuck because why stress when he is able to enjoy free time for the first time in years.

For soap opera fans, in the end, he found a better job with much better pay, met the person of his life, got married and lived happily forever after.

5. Your fear of not having a hot body

You have a big butt and worry that it might get spanked in public? You think nobody will date you if your boobs aren't the size of watermelons? You think going bald was the end of your dating life?

If you can make changes about your appearance, weight, butt, or whatever, do it instead of moaning about it. When you compare yourself to others, you are feeding your insecurities and making it harder to come to terms with yourself and your body.

There was once my friend Bobby who tried for years to prevent hair loss to the extent that he wore a toupee everywhere. One very windy day, his toupee flew off and onto the lap of a woman sitting on a bench. Embarrassed, he slowly walked away, only for the lady to tell him how much better he looked without it. At that moment, he defied his fears by setting fire to the wig and never gave a fuck again.

6. Old friends who never talk to you

We have all kinds of friends: childhood friends, work-friends, college-friends, etc. As we grow older, we may linger on maintaining friendships due to nostalgic reasons, but the truth is, they may not be who you remember them to be. They may not even care about you or always be too busy to spend five minutes with you.

Holding on to the hope that someone you once knew still wants to hang out leads to you evaluating yourself negatively. You probably think that you aren't good enough and then you try even harder. Why not just stop giving a fuck, at least then you can focus valuable time on yourself.

Berger McDonald

7. Family members who think they know you

It doesn't matter how successful you are when it comes to family, they can't seem to shake off their pre-conceived opinion that you haven't changed. Your mom still thinks you listen to nirvana and your dad thinks you are still dating a girl you met in high-school.

These tedious opinions can deflate your ego to the point where you have to act different around your family. Instead, stop giving a fuck. It's time they are the ones that need to grow up, not you!

8. Being single

You go to a dinner party hosted by all your married friends, all in relationships except you. You know at one point, someone is going to ask the dreaded question, 'are you seeing anyone yet?'

You might not know this now but being single is okay and you will meet someone eventually. What happens when somebody rushes into a relationship is disastrous, but since their need to feel loved and show the world they are loved, they are too often willing to sacrifice their mental wellbeing by dating a complete douche?

Instead of doing that, focus on the beautiful things a single life is giving you, and enjoy every minute of it.

9. Social media and social status

The technological advancements of today have replaced many of our needs, some good and some terrible. Every time we get a notification on social media, our brains reward us with endorphins, thus making us happy.

But, make a post on Facebook, and go five minutes without a comment or like and OMG, you think nobody likes you, and the world is going to end.

Remember, having 5000 friends on Facebook is no equivalent to having 2 or 3 best friends in real life.

10.   Every other little thing in everyday life

Imagine going to work one morning and as you leave the house it begins to rain AND you forgot your umbrella. Your day is ruined right?

Not entirely, not when you don't give a fuck instead. Once you get to work, tell everyone how silly you were and see the funny side of it. It's harder to work towards having a good day if it starts off wrong, so try and alter your perspective in a way that isn't going to lead to you crying yourself to sleep after a long and horrible day.

Categorize your Fucks in to the List

"I remember my mom saying, 'I will take you to every audition, I will support you, but the minute you stop caring about it, I will stop.'" — *Justin Timberlake, ex-boyfriend of Britney Spears and okay dancer.*

At this moment you should already have a clear idea of what bothersome issue is plaguing your life. There is probably more than one as a matter of fact.

So in order to avoid 'giving a fuck' so many times in your life, you need to categorize them into a list and have a plan in place to act accordingly when things happen, and therefore, handle them more effectively.

For example, if your biggest problem is your mother-in-law, getting her a one way plane ticket to Antarctica is the first option for most guys. But it's not a permanent solution and would only cause more problems. Unless you can send her to the moon, of course, that's a differently story.

Joking aside, I know you love your mother-in-law and so do I.

So, how do you categorize your fucks? Follow the steps below and get them organized into a list.

Step 1:

Make a strong cup of coffee, turn off your phone, i.e. pretend you are dead. Figure out your most pressing concern or issue. If you are unsure, think about what keeps you awake at night. Make a list of things that you can do something about now and things you can do at a later date. Prioritize your list from hard to easy.

And stop fucking procrastinating, at this point you are probably already back to binge-watching on Netflix or watching cat videos.

Prepare yourself for the next few changes you have planned, the ones that can't happen overnight. Look into what skills and experiences you have developed over the years and reflect on this, you have come far little hobbit.

Set a timer or wake yourself up with an impromptu cold shower, throw your phone out the window even. Use this available time to get rid of things you don't need.

Step 2:

Produce a calendar and write the things you can change on those dates, or write what you hope to achieve on those dates. For the things you can change today, get to it! Here are a few ideas to help:

- For friends who always let you down; tell them you are sick of their shit and give them an ultimatum.

- For a job you hate; put in your notice now!

- For a partner who doesn't appreciate your awesomeness; explain that you are making some changes in your life and you can't wait for them.

- For losing weight or anything about your body; check your weight, then have a beer.

If you are having difficulty with not giving a fuck, remind yourself why you should pursue it. If you usually spend 20 minutes to get ready to go out, opt to wear no make-up instead and use that valuable time on something more productive.

If you tend to be the voice of reason of your 'friend circle,' you are already in the position where you have to spend time listening to their problems or giving advice, whereas if you stop giving a fuck, you can just direct them to the next best listener.

Step 3:

Remind yourself that anything that involves pain, sweat and frustration is probably worth your time, and worth your fucks. You can't make an omelet without breaking an egg. Staying focused during this transition is a testament to your determination and willpower. It is do or don't, not maybe or maybe not.

Continue working through the list, and document any positive outcomes to further reinforce your stance. A few things will occur once you have successfully completed one or all items on the list:

- You will notice that it wasn't as difficult as you initially thought.

- You will notice that people are giving you more attention or respect.

- You will notice you have more self-confidence and drive.

Presentation, practice, production

I worked as an English teacher in Asia for four years, and in that time, lessons were structured on the PPP teaching method, (Presentation, Practice, Production). This method of learning can also be applied to any given situation or fuck. Let's do an example.

Gabe is dishing out way too many fucks in his life. He's stressed from his job, and constantly feels that his managers are pressuring him too much with emails, and he never has time for anything else.

Okay Gabe, put your fucks into a list and let's see what you can do.

- Managers at work are dicks.

- Never has time for anything.

- Stresses too much.

Now, let's stop giving a generous fuck. Try this instead.

- Introduce a system where managers can only delegate work at specific times, otherwise you can't or won't do it.

- This system should free up more time for you to focus on other stuff.

- You don't need to worry about getting extra work.

Okay, now practice this and the end result could be:

- Increased productivity during the period of time you set.

- Managers stop being dicks.

- Less stress, more free time.

It is possible the managers thought you were someone they could walk over, or that you had unlimited fucks to dish out. Don't get me wrong, making such an assertion at work isn't easy and it could very easily backfire. However, NO RISK, NO REWARD!

Chapter 3: Facing Fear and Accepting Your Vulnerabilities

Anytime you ask someone what their biggest fear is, there are usually one of three answers:

- Death

- Spiders

- Clowns

Is that really it? You can avoid clowns and spiders, but death is unavoidable so there is no point in worrying about it. A random healthy man might even die in his sleep tonight.

Overcoming the fear of our inevitable death can lead into learning about other, more hidden, established fears that you CAN do something about.

To set the wheels in motion, acknowledge your fears, overcome them, and then work towards not giving a fuck. Here a few ideas.

Don't always assume the worst

When we think in a fearful way, it attracts more fear. Aim to not automatically expect the worst, and train your mind to expect the best. Make positive assumptions about the future.

Don't give time or energy to fear

When an adventurous thrill-seeker bungee jumps, do they wait around thirty minutes or do they just take the plunge? Try to have the same mindset when it comes to what you fear. If you are afraid to tell someone how you feel—for example, how much of a dick they are—the longer you wait, the more stressed you are before doing it.

Be prepared and ready, not taking action because of your fear means opportunities could be passing you by.

Don't dwell on scarcity

Live as if you are the richest person in the world, not in the sense of cash, but celebrate what you have and be willing to help others out when you can, as there is no better feeling.

Live vicariously through the success of your friends and family

When a friend opens a restaurant and tells you about it with excitement, do you tell them 'great news' or do you jump into a taxi for the first opening?

These situations can really motivate you and make you appreciate the people you have in your life.

Plan on becoming great

Ultimately, if you really want to face your fears, there needs to be an end-goal, something to drive you towards achieving it. Calculate possible risks and learn how to break through any obstacles if you don't know how already.

Feeling empowered yet? Feeling like you couldn't give a fuck about many of the things life craps out onto you? Next up is looking at dealing with certain aspects of life with the 'don't give a fuck' mentality because not giving a fuck is staring down life's challenges, yet taking action regardless.

Chapter 4: The Pain in the ass that is work

We spend most of our life working. So work is undoubtedly the place that causes us a lot of stress, and gives us so many fucks. So it should be evident that work is one of the first places to start out not giving a fuck.

Dealing with meetings

Meetings at work are ALWAYS fun, in fact, the only way they would be even more fun is if everyone is dressed as a clown.

Let's look into the general process of a meeting and then cross-analyze it with your newly found attitude.

When you gave a fuck at a meeting

Moments before the meeting begins, you are in a panic, asking everyone if they know what it's all about. You're trying to retain your composure, but you are sweating profusely and might even piss yourself if your boss says your name more than once.

Everyone is herded in like sheep, and once the boss sits down then everyone else is allowed to sit down too. Ideas start flooding your mind with negative thoughts. "Oh fuck, my performance was shit this week," is what you think to yourself while maintaining a frozen grin to disguise your fear.

The boss starts talking, first telling an unfunny joke, then everyone else laughs hysterically, their heads tipped so far back they look like pelicans gulping a 12-inch subway sandwich. You join in too but laugh even harder, hitting your hand on the table to emphasize how 'funny' the joke was.

The boss pulls up some statistics and plans for next week, and there is lots of pointing. Everyone is nodding in unison, making optimistic "mmm" sounds. You are still scared at some point that you are in the line of fire, even though it's got nothing to do with you.

Co-workers make notes and you enjoy a sigh of relief as the meeting ends. "Another week safe," you think to yourself.

Does it sound like your meeting at work? If so, then how about don't give a fuck?

When you don't give a fuck at a meeting

You wait patiently outside, wondering what to do after work. Everyone is herded in, you sit down comfortably, not opting for the fetal position like your co-workers.

The boss tells a joke, you smile a little but then decide to interject with a better joke. You get a standing ovation (probably) and promotion (maybe). Boss comes over and gives you a high-5, as co-workers hold back tears since their years of brown-nosing has yet to get them noticed.

Meeting is finished, boss asks you to stay behind and wants to learn more about you.

Types of co-workers and when to not give a fuck about them

Regardless of the field of work you do, there is always an array of co-workers to deal with, some great and some not so great. Understanding the different types of co-workers is essential to learning how to react to them, deal with them and, ultimately, not give a fuck about them.

The gossip

How might they affect you?

The gossip assumes that their main job duty involves talking about other people, the only thing that gives them pleasure is relaying the latest scandal regardless of the level of consistency to it. Their favorite pastimes include, but are not limited to; dropping hints, ruining reputations and listening in on conversations.

You know the day will come that you will be the target and have to tiptoe around work, afraid that you are being judged, but not even sure why.

What to do about it:

Gossips crave attention! So if they start talking about you, why not confront them during a meeting or hide the boss in a filing cupboard and encourage the gossip to talk about how silly the boss's tie is, and then he can burst out screeching, "How dare you!"

Alternatively (and simpler) is to just ignore the gossip. Aim to never tell them anything about your personal life. The less attention the gossip gets, the less power they have.

When you walk by, gaze into their eyes with a frozen smile as this reflects how their opinion has no power over you.

The slacker

How might they affect you?

There's always one person at work who seems to literally do nothing, and even when they are given a task, they attempt to delegate it to someone else. The slacker is skilled in the art of deception, and at any moment will blame someone else for a mistake. This can include you.

What to do about it:

Gather Intel and evidence on the slacker and keep it somewhere safe. In today's economic climate, jobs aren't as safe as they once were, so you need to safeguard yourself. Knowing you have some evidence gathered for a worst case scenario means that you can relax and stop worrying about the slacker.

The brown-noser

How might they affect you?

The brown-noser is a co-worker who dedicates their entire waking life to sucking up to the boss. They are usually so far up the boss's ass that when the boss yawns, everyone can see their face. The major problem with this co-worker is that they are stealing the spotlight from all the other hard-workers, they tend to boast about how "the boss" let them drink his 20-year old aged whiskey, (the very same age as their cheap floozies).

You won't get a promotion anytime soon if the brown-noser is blocking the way.

What to do about it:

The brown-noser lacks any other skills apart from providing compliments to the boss, you 'could' do it too, but chances are you are probably way better than them at your work. Talk to the boss and ask if he needs assistance in anything or request feedback on your work so you can improve.

At the end of the day, what is most important at work is

work. What the boss cares most about is productivity. Suddenly the brown-noser doesn't seem worth a moment of the boss's time anymore. What have you got to lose?

The Complainer

How might they affect you?

Most jobs have ups and downs but if someone at work is constantly complaining, it makes the environment and general morale at work much more difficult. The complainer is someone who moans all the time that nothing ever works right, or any time there is a new change, they already have their negative opinions on it.

If you already hate your job or strongly dislike it, the complainer is only there to remind you every second that you are there.

What to do about it:

Ignore them. When they complain, talk about the positive side of things. The complainers crave attention and love it when you moan with them. Ignoring their complaints long enough will give them the idea that you're no longer worth their time and they will move on to the next person that will be more likely to join in the moaning with them.

TMI Sharer

How might they affect you?

Just got laid last night for fifth time in a row? Spotted their first grey pube? Wife is having an affair? This co-worker won't spare you the gritty details of their life, they don't seem to even have a limit on how far they are willing to go to tell you everything.

Occasionally, it's entertaining, however, it's also not professional and after some time, you will try to avoid this co-worker as much as possible, causing tension and conflict.

What to do about it:

You are not the only one offended by their level of honesty, all you need to do is politely ask if they could tell you all the details in a more suitable environment, such as outside of work. They just won't know that you never plan on meeting them outside of work.

The dinosaur

How might they affect you?

The dinosaur has been around since the company started using computers instead of typewriters. The dinosaur has seen everything and aren't hesitant to mention how much things have changed since their day.

What to do about it:

Surprisingly the dinosaur is a useful source of information about the company and how to get ahead. They know the names of all the important managers and how to get to them if ever you fantasized about moving up in the ranks. If you can learn to tolerate their ancient mind, then you can learn about their ancient ways. It's a win-win.

The passive-aggressive civil war and bullying

Are you finding post-it notes surrounding your desk when you arrive in the morning? Are the notes telling you how to do your job, but you don't know who they are from? Found a dead animal or fresh turd in your drawer?

Sounds like you got yourself a passive-aggressive co-worker!

To fully understand whether or not you are in a warzone, consider the following about another co-worker:

- Doing less when asked for more.

- Missing deadlines and then not caring.

- Withholding important information stating that, "It's confidential, motherfucker."

- Leaving tacky notes or using e-mail to avoid face-to-face confrontation.

- Ignoring any notes or e-mails left by others.

- Communicating only via emoji's or pigeon language.

- Complaining about everything from office policies to procedures.

- Arriving late and not taking any ownership.

- Extending their lunch break without permission.

- "Forgetting" or "misplacing" important documents.

- Resisting suggestions for change or improvement.

- Procrastinating or recording everything on their phones.

- Not holding in farts, especially during important presentations or when bad news is announced.

- Calling out coworkers in public settings, such as meetings or during presentations.

- Writing mean things on the companies twitter page.

- Stealing food from the refrigerator when it's been clearly marked with someone's name.

- Starting emails using a first name only.

If you are experiencing any or all of the following from a co-worker, then it's a warzone! Now, you are probably wondering what to do and how not giving a fuck comes into it. Here's what to do:

Objective 1: Identify that the co-worker is making your life hell and remind yourself that their pathetic attempts to unhinge you are not going to work. The more they try to get a response from you, the more you should refrain from interacting.

Objective 2: Catch the culprit out on their bullshit or anytime you are forced to engage, insinuate that their behavior or snarky remarks are actually compliments. Smile when they are sarcastic to you and wait until you get home to cry when they hurt your feelings.

Passive-aggressive co-worker: *"Have you put on weight?"*

You: *"I've been doing a lot of squats recently, I guess it's working because you noticed my ass. Thanks!"*

Objective 3: Suppress any frustration or angry feelings about the co-worker, their disingenuous comments should deflect off you as if you were Superman. Eventually they should give up because they realize their power is useless against you.

Objective 4: Extend the olive branch to your co-worker when you feel it's the right time and that they have given up their preposterous efforts to undermine you. Establish that while you both don't need to be friends, you don't need to be enemies either and can work together with a mutual respect. If a truce is not on the cards, use this opportunity to explain that further passive-aggressive behavior will not be tolerated.

Objective 5: Report the person to a manager if or when things cross the line, such as instead of finding one piece of used underwear on your seat, it's now a matching pair. Think about unlawful territory or harassment so threatening that simply not giving a fuck is no longer an option. At this point, you need to give a fuck, eek! Report behavior to a supervisor immediately if it affects your job duties.

Paperwork and dress code

It's a Friday night, you are one hour away from finishing, and the excitement of spending the weekend away from work is urging you to maximize your output 100 times faster than any other day of the week. Then suddenly, the manager or other subordinate drops a pile of work on your desk, accompanied with a sinister smirk.

You have to change your arrangements with friends, telling them you can't go out tonight and maybe even all weekend. Fuck!

Now, you might assume there is nothing you can do about it, right? Let's try the situation again but with the "don't give a fuck" attitude.

As soon as the manager approaches, stop them in their tracks! Inform them that you are already loaded with work and anything added to your to-do pile will only end in misery. Intimidated that you have balls, there is a chance that since they are in a higher position and feel ever so important, they may believe that you have no right to question their authority. At this moment, emphasize how indifferent you are and how you intend for things to change, otherwise, you can very easily find another job

AND it would be their responsibility to explain to the boss just how and why such a great employee left.

If you're afraid of your manager and even more afraid to say no to them, then you are giving too many fucks. If you limit their control over you by not giving a fuck and more importantly, by showing them you don't give a fuck, then your reward is more time and less stress.

Here are a few other ways you can learn to not give a fuck when it involves paperwork:

• Become more vocal at work; explain how your company's competitors don't even use paper anymore, decreasing the carbon footprint or whatever environmentally-friendly fad is popular. In fact, the only time you should see paper at work is in the toilet.

• Introduce recording notes instead of writing them down. The astonished dinosaurs at work (who only joined social media last week) will try to downplay your idea until you point out the benefits. If they still seem hesitant, explain how all the big companies out there are already doing it.

• Get organized! Create a simple filing system and set-up colored files or folders for different things. You could also set-up a few baskets to make work life a little easier, such as a to-do basket, a to-read basket, a to-file basket, a to-pay basket, and anything else should go into the trash bin, or recycling.

• If you have a pile of work to complete, encourage that new intern to do some of it for you. One great trick is to ask for a favor you know that is out of reach, then when you ask for something less, they feel more obliged to help. For example:

You: *"Hey, new intern!"*

Intern: *"My name is Tiffany."*

You: *"Okay, Brittany. Can I borrow $100?"*

Intern: *"I don't have that kind of money, I still live at home."*

You: *"Ah shucks, well, could you put these files of clients surnames into alphabetical order instead. It's only a few thousand. I believe in you!"*

Intern: *"Absolutely! Finally some responsibilities other than making coffee all day."*

You: *"Oh, yeah, and I'll need a coffee too."*

Remember that for things you can't control, you shouldn't stress, but if you can make subtle changes in regards to paperwork to make life just that little bit easier then do it. DO IT NOW!

Why do we need a dress code at work? The possible reasons are:

- As a reminder that you belong to that company, and to discourage abstract thought or opinion.

- Your dreams and hopes for the future are only encouraged by having a choice in what you wear, and thus a risk to the company that one day you might even leave.

- You will work more effectively by abiding to a dress code.

Of course, most companies aren't that strict, they might even let you dress up for Halloween or Christmas. Once a year is reasonable, right?

What bothers us the most about a dress code? Does it remind us of high school? Do you think it's okay that only the boss can wear a Spiderman tie but nobody else? That if your skirt is once inch higher, you are immediately classed as a slut?

Katrina was starting a new job as a secretary. On her first day, within minutes of starting, she gets called into a meeting about her attire. The boss explains that her skirt is too much of too little. Katrina, who didn't give a fuck, then enquired, "Do you happen to have a replacement skirt, maybe something from the 1950s?" At that moment, the boss felt awkward and could see where Katrina was coming from, (and totally missed that she was being sarcastic). From that point onwards, she could dress however she liked because she was confident in her job and confident in herself, so confident as to question the boss on the first day.

Peter got a job teaching English in Thailand. He was on the other side of the world and the head teacher told him that he needed to shave his beard.

"What does having a beard got to do with how I do my job? Should I be penalized just because none of the other guys can't grow one?"

The head teacher couldn't explain herself, and she only

said, *"Because it looks polite."*

Peter stated *"It takes me months to grow this beast, it's not going away."*

Did he lose his job because he didn't give a fuck? No, if anything he was very popular with the kids because they had never seen anyone like him before.

It's so easy to get caught up in the idea of losing your job by not following every order, but then you sacrifice so much about yourself too. Is it your dream job? Is it worth your time and effort to really do everything they want? Is it a stepping stone, a job you don't intend on working for too long, just until you have enough money to invest in something else or go travel?

- The point is, there are so many working conditions in jobs that things such as dress codes shouldn't be on the top of the agenda, (unless you live somewhere like Saudi Arabia). So don't give a fuck if:

- You have to wear socks with no patterns.

- You can't grow a beard.

- Your skirt is too high.

- You have to wear a jacket.

- You have to wear a red tie on Mondays, blue on Tuesday...

- Anything else that is widely considered ludicrous.

Your mental wellbeing is what's important, not some draconian rules about your image or the fear of being judged based on your personal appearance.

Chapter 5: The joys of family and how to not give a fuck when needed

Family are ALWAYS concerned about you, concerned that:

- You still work part-time.

- You still aren't married.

- You still don't know how to iron a shirt.

- You still smoke.

- You still go partying after the age of 30.

- You look like you are going bald.

- You got a tattoo.

- You got your nipples pierced and didn't tell them until years later.

- You broke up with your partner and forgot to tell them.

- Your car smells like fart soup.

- You are always late.

- You stopped believing in God.

- You stopped believing in politics.

- You stopped believing in monogamy.

- And much, much more!

And you are concerned that if they at least bothered to add you to social media, they would be up to date with every aspect of your life that occurs when you aren't spending every second with them.

Approaching opinionated family members without using violence

As much as you would love to punch your racist grandpa, you know that it's not going to happen. His false teeth will just pop out and he will cackle, stating you "punch like a pussy." You NEED to learn other ways to overcome the situations with family that you know are going to aggravate and upset you.

How can this be achieved, you wonder? Do you remind them of their own failings in life? Do you pretend you can't hear them and just nod politely from a distance? There's a much simpler way—not giving a fuck.

Try to focus on the positives

Instead of stressing about how a family member irritates or frustrates you, remind yourself about things or qualities that you like about them. Grandpa farts all the time and occasionally wets himself, however his classic stories of the war only endear you to him further.

You expect your mother to nag you about being single, but at least she's willing to cook you a meal and give you a hug after losing a game of Scrabble.

Prepare yourself

Think about possible questions that you normally plan on avoiding, envision how your next interaction with your goal-orientated sister could potentially play out.

If she's going to spew out all of her latest successes and weight loss, offer a high-5 or a business handshake (a strong and firm handshake). Suddenly the self-righteous go from smug to shrug, and her overly inflated ego deflates in seconds.

Give out a healthy dose of empathy

Understanding other family member's perspectives can help you in dealing with them. You don't need to agree with everything they say or do, but just by giving a little empathy you can make the annual family gatherings a lot more tolerable, shit, maybe even enjoyable. If you think that your uncle dishes out irrelevant advice, understand that he's probably coming from someone with bad relationships and that's his way of dealing with it.

What to say to family members to show you don't give a fuck

Even though you can mentally prepare yourself before meeting family, figuring out what to say isn't as easy.

You can't always avoid annoying Auntie Annie, especially when she thinks it's perfectly okay to tell you that when she was your age, she was already married with three kids. Who gives a fuck? Not you!

When you feel an argument is about to erupt

Take blame off of the other person by using "I" statements. Instead of, "you are talking shit," try, "I feel like you are talking shit." By referring to yourself, this helps lighten the conversation and is a nice way of showing you don't give a fuck. Try a few practice sentences in front of a mirror:

"I feel that this is not something that interests me."

"I don't think that's going to help my current situation."

"I am going to acknowledge your advice but I can't promise that I won't ignore it regardless."

Offer a choice

When a family member is offending you or refuses to change the topic, explain that you are tired of the discussion and that if they are not willing to change the topic then you will politely leave... or dropkick them in the face.

Use a gentle tone to set limits

A big family feast involves one or two relations thinking they can control everything and disregard everyone else's opinion (like a horny peacock). Introduce a few limits in a friendly tone such as, "I like your idea, however, I also have an idea so let's figure out a way for both of us to work together."

Suggest that it's time for a break

Feel like the discussion is heading towards a cat fight or jelly wrestling tournament? Too many alpha males throwing their weight about? Things getting more intense than an episode of Oprah in 3D? It's time for a break. Usher everyone inside or outside or into a basement to calm the situation down. If you feel as if your conversation is going to get to be too much, explain you are going outside for a cigarette (even though you don't smoke) or just for some fresh air.

Put the conversation on hold

If it's too overwhelming to discuss your single life with your parents, explain that it's getting to be too much and you would rather discuss it another time, preferably when you've had time to get drunk first.

Other things to consider

- Keep gatherings with family short, don't plan on spending an entire day with a person who will have more opportunities to annoy the shit out of you.

- Avoid religious and political topics in conversation, this usually ends in turmoil and aggression. If a family member insists in talking about it, go to another room.

- Change or avoid situations that causes family members to piss you off. If your mother hates when you come into the house with dirty shoes, enter through a window.

- Take deep breaths when you are feeling overwhelmed, ground yourself and repeat the mantra "don't give a fuck, don't give a fuck, don't give a fuck..."

- Remember how not to react with your behavior, if it's difficult to ignore a family member, pause for a moment and think about how you can prevent an argument.

What if your family don't like your partner

Eventually at some point, you are going to have to introduce your partner to your family and this doesn't go as smooth as pouring a glass of delicious white wine. You parents or family have pre-meditated questions ready to sling out once your partner is seated comfortably, questions they couldn't find from a simple Google search or after spending several days stalking your partner's social media.

Possible questions may include:

- What do you do for a living?

- What religion are you?

- What did you study at college?

- Does pineapple go on the pizza or not?

- Do you plan on having children?

- Do you already have children?

- What's your blood type?

- Do you have any pre-existing medical conditions?

- How would you rate the last Star Wars movie?

- Since you don't have a college degree, which McDonald's branch do you work in?

With so many quick-fire questions, your partner is going to shy away from discussion, since being put on a 'peddle-stool' can relinquish a person's self-esteem and confidence in unfamiliar surroundings. It's time to not give a fuck and put your family straight.

Find out what the problem is

There have been countless romance movies where the partner's parents make it increasingly difficult for true love to blossom. Think of iconic movies such as dirty dancing, clueless, and E.T. for example.

The fact is, there is a pressing matter or problem that you need to get to the bottom to. You should know your family better than anyone, but in case they are keeping quiet for fear of upsetting you, you'll need to ask a few questions.

Usually in these situations, they are making false assumptions of your partner based on ignorance or lack of information, and thus are resolved with a simple history lesson or explanation about your partner.

Advocate for your partner

Seeing as your family members aren't in your relationship, they aren't aware of all the experiences and good times that have happened during said relationship. It's easy for family members to remind you of failed past affiliations and how you've been hurt, but it's a new relationship, new you, new everything.

Drive home all the great things about your partner, how they let you eat pizza in bed, how they don't beat you with a broom if you leave the toilet seat up, how they let you watch scary movies past your bedtime.

At this point, your family should have retracted their view and possibly even apologized. If not, tell them how you don't give a fuck. If they aren't willing to make the effort to get to know your partner, then you can use that time more productively with your significant other.

Support your partner and give them an insight into your family

It can take time, and it's okay. Give your partner a bit more insight into your family and elaborate on reasons why they are being such raging douchebags.

Sometimes you just need to create a connection between your partner and your family to help dampen your family's opinion of your partner. A great way is karaoke, everybody loves Abba, after all, everybody!

Find ways for your partner to become more involved with your family. Putting up a shelf or helping cook a big dinner are great ideas.

Don't give a fuck when no matter how hard you try, you just can't seem to convince your family that you are happy and that's what matters.

Chapter 6: Friends and when to give a fuck

Different types of friends in your life

During the early stage of life, we happen to have a bunch of friends, once we grow up, go to college and develop a personality, we gather even more. Sociologists believe friendships thrive based on three conditions:

1. Proximity; repeated.

2. Unplanned interactions.

3. A setting that encourages people to let their guard down and confide in each other.

After school ends, friends tend to break out into more distinct tiers. It would look a little like this:

1. Top tier: this is you.

2. Tier 1: closest friends.

3. Tier 2: good friends.

4. Tier 3: acquaintances.

5. Bottom of tier: complete strangers.

Tier 1 friends

Friends in this category are treated like a brother or sister, if you were to get married tomorrow, these are the friends you would depend on to make arrangements and deliver important speeches about you, (with a few tales of debauchery thrown in for good measure).

Friendships in this tier are usually based from childhood, high school or college, basically a long time of ups, downs, tests, trials and secrets.

Your closest friends are least likely to get upset with you over small things, or even big ones for that matter.

Tier 2 friends

Friends in this category are not as reliable as tier 1 friends, however there is still the trust element and you could contact them at any moment without feeling awkward or having to use small talk first.

Friendships in this tier are usually based on work friends, friends you made during travels, ex's from past relationships, friends you made during your hobbies. Enough time to understand each other enough and spend a considerable amount of time communicating.

If your good friends are pissed off about something, there is no surefire way of guaranteeing that they will tell you, making things lead further into disarray.

Tier 3 friends

These are people who you are friends with on social media and occasionally talk to if you see them in public.

Sometimes they are friends of friends or neighbors or your friends' partner, etc. You don't necessarily need them in your life and they can easily fade back into strangers over time.

Complete strangers

You should know what a stranger is, if you don't recognize them, then you don't know them. Though at some point, all of your friends were strangers so the opportunity to make friends is always there, I guess it depends on the situation. Could you see yourself becoming best friends with the local parish priest because they share a passion for rollerblading? Quite possibly yes.

So, understanding the different types of friends in your life is imperative to how many fucks you can give.

How many fucks do you give to a stranger who's rude to you on the bus? Zero.

How about a close friend who's pissed you forgot their birthday? Maybe 2 fucks, 3 to make things better.

Questions to ask before giving a fuck

Okay, so you know a shit ton of people in your life but how do you decide who is worth your time, effort and general awesomeness. Ask yourself the following questions when making such an important decision:

- Is this someone you get excited to meet once a week or even in a month?

- Do you see them playing an important role in your future?

- Would you drop whatever you are doing to go support them in a crisis?

- Would they lend you money? Like a little, not a million.

- Is this someone who you love having around your family and partner?

- Does this person encourage new ideas, and adventures, and gives you tips when you need them most?

- Do they offer to be a wingman on a night out?

- Do they make you laugh so much you pee a little bit?

- Can you trust them?

- Do they introduce you to other quality people in life?

- And last but not least, would they cry at your funeral?

Friendships are different to other relationships in that you choose to have someone in your life and regardless of whether they are close or good friends, when shit hits the fan, you expect them to be there, and vice versa.

If they seem pissed off, upset, frustrated or whatever with you, you need to give a fuck about it. Prioritize them and make things right, the older we get, and the fewer friends we have to rely on and tell us when we are being a big douche.

Chapter 7: The magic of not giving a fuck

How not giving a fuck benefits you

Concerned citizens of the world will tell you how not giving a fuck is bad, real bad. As if you are just giving up on life as you know it and that everything that matters to you is irrelevant.

You know what's really irrelevant though? The small, trivial things in life that seem to just excruciate the fuck out of you. That's what you are not giving a fuck about, the drama, the constant weight-loss ads fucking everywhere you blink, the person you go on a date with and the first thing they tell you is that they are gluten-free and not their name.

Do you have time for all that? Because it all adds up. All that valuable time wasted being pissed off about such stupid things.

As we get older, we become more selective in handing out the fucks. We come to the conclusion that time isn't on our side anymore, that whatever use to hold us back shouldn't even if that includes people.

There was once an Israeli entrepreneur who spent a

solid year designing a selfie-stick that could also be used as a smartphone cover. Less than a week of putting it out there on a crowdfunding website, Chinese designers replicated both the design and concept, and completely ruined his chances of fame and fortune. What happened after that? Well, he learned to not give a fuck, because lightning speed Chinese copycats are something he has no control over. The entrepreneur still carried on with his product and made it a success, utilizing the fact that he got cheated as a way to crowdsource further.

Giving less fucks opens you up to more opportunity!

Did you ever hear about the book that taught parrot owners how to train their parrots to talk? The author was an average guy with an idea, he couldn't sleep each night without thinking about it and thinking about how handy this book would be to fellow parrot owners. So he wrote a book, detailing how to train your parrot to talk. You probably thought you wouldn't give a fuck about that, right? He sold millions of copies worldwide.

He had an idea and wasn't pressured into NOT pursuing it, and that's the general gist of this book. It's so simple to passively ignore your own capabilities and skills without realizing that you actually don't have anything to lose and don't need to give a fuck.

Chapter 8: Get the monkey off your back!

So, you probably wonder about the cover of this book.

Seriously, what does this good looking dude handing out a banana have to do with a book about not giving a fuck?

Well, ever heard of a term, "having a monkey on your back"? It means that you're carrying a burden—a monkey—on your back all the time and it's difficult to get rid of it.

When you learn not to give a fuck, you are ready to get rid of that monkey. Set yourself free to a better, stress-free life.

But the problem is that you will find more often than not, you're carrying other people's monkey, too.

I remembered Peter, a buddy, ran into me one day, complaining about the girl he has a crush on that doesn't seem to care a bit about him despite all the efforts he made to impress her. I gave him some tips to help him impress the girl. My dating strategies for him went to my bed that night. I was thinking, "If he can do this, and I can help him do this, then maybe we can get this," then I realized, "Oh my God, I'm taking his monkey!" Why am I worried about his dating problem when I have a dating problem of my own, not to mention a full list of so many other problems to deal with?

At that moment, in my mind, I told Peter, "Here is the banana for your monkey, and here is your monkey back. I love you, but sorry, I don't give a fuck…"

You will find that in your life, you will unconsciously take on people's monkeys from time to time. When you realize it, hand them a banana for their monkey, and give the monkey back.

Chapter 9: When to give a fuck

Now you know how to not give a fuck.

Then do you ever need to actually give a fuck? Absolutely.

Go back to your fuck list in chapter 2. And if you face something that's not on your fuck list, take a moment and evaluate it to see if it's worth giving a fuck for.

If it's about someone you love, then hell yeah, give it a fuck or two.

If it's about your health, such as exercising, hell yeah, get your ass off the couch and give it three fucks.

If it's about your self-improvement, go all the way for

it.

It's so easy to want a carefree life, have a pet Chihuahua and make some money. It's too easy. Ask yourself instead, "What are you willing to fight for? To struggle with?"

Ask yourself, evaluate your life, give a fuck when need be, and most importantly, know how to not give a fuck!

Conclusion

Life isn't easy, sometimes it's horrible and unpredictable and you think, "What's the point?"

Don't think you're alone, there's a lot of suffering out there. The point is, what are YOU going to do about it? Hiding in a basement and hoping it goes away doesn't count as not giving a fuck.

You can see in many aspects of your life such as family, work, relationships, friends, etc., you have the power to control how to react and act in different situations. You understand now that by taking action and refusing indifference, the long term rewards are worth it. Better relationships, better working conditions, better sex drive, all these are within reach and all you had to do was acknowledge the fucks and the don't give a fucks.

Whether it's something small such as telling a friend to

stop tagging you in drunk photos, or something big such as setting the wheels in motion to learn to drive a monster truck, by facing any fear through not giving a fuck, you are developing a mindset that will change your future for the rest of your life.

I hope that this book help you know exactly when to not give a fuck, so you can enjoy your life to the fullest!

Final Words

Thank you so much for reading this book.

I hope you enjoyed it and know how to not give a fuck now.

Send it as a gift to someone you love and let them know how to not give a fuck and enjoy their lives too!

If you liked the book, would you do me a huge favor and write a review on Amazon?

Your review is really important and it will help others know what to expect from this book.

It will really encourage me to write more books for you.

I look forward to reading your review.

Also, read or listen to my other humorous book "50 Awesome Things to Do in Retirement". Even if you're not retired yet, you should definitely check it out and be prepared. Warning: it's not like anything you would normally think it is...

Thank you so much. Now get out there, enjoy your life and let others know that you don't give a fuck.

Bye for now, good luck, and take care!

Berger McDonald

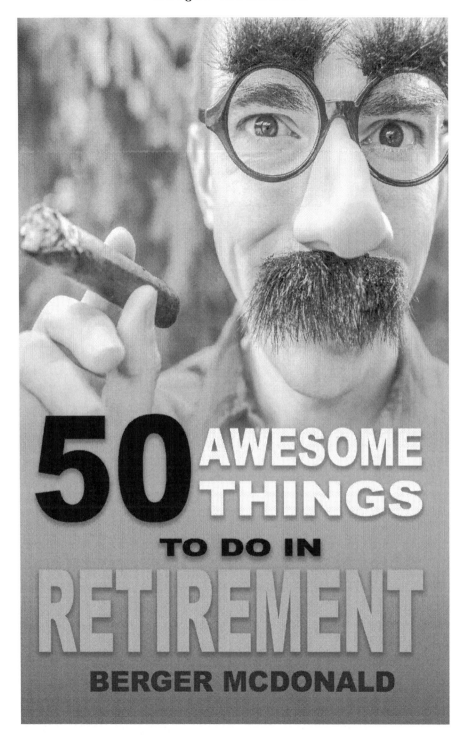

19805693R10066

Printed in Great Britain
by Amazon